SUPER V

Kuckaburro

~ *Va te faire foutre* ~

Psychobabble

El Dorado

Seal Pup

Cannibal Chicken

I Should've Never Left the House

U.G.L.Y

Baby I Love You

Crack Cocaine

Hey Big

F.U.K.P.O.D

Smoke Dope

V.D.

21st Century Redneck

Burnt-Monkey's?

COWORKER!!

Party! Party! Party!

Introduction / Eulogy / Explanation

What started as three friends and a notebook became the side project that couldn't be, then was, now never to continue. Let me explain: I am Jeff Worley. My brother Chris and I have played in the rock band Jackyl for over 25 years. We tour so much that I am probably on stage a somewhere as you are reading this right now! When Jackyl was up and coming our friend James "Virgil" Hamilton was our biggest fan. Virgil was a combination of Liberace, Rambo, and James Brown. I say *was* because sadly Virgil has passed on to the big stage in the sky. We had been friends since childhood so let me correct myself; he was not our biggest fan, he was our biggest FANATIC. After cheering us on for many years Virgil approached me one day with the idea of writing some songs together. He handed me a notebook filled with something in between lyrics, poetry, and confessions from the soul. I'll be honest here, I did not expect too much from this, but he surprised me. To preface this, Virgil did not really have that much musical ability, it would be my brother Chris and I that would bring that. Virgil had something different, something so special that one could not learn it, you must be born with it. Virgil had pure, untamed, raw emotion that caused him great pain when he kept it inside and I knew this. Finding myself with some time off and exploding with creativity, I talked to my brother and we thought, "What the hell?". One thing about Virgil you need to know: In a good old southern expression my grandmother used to say, "That boy was a handful". To be honest my brother and I had just built a recording studio and we needed some new material to experiment with the gear. What happened next, I never thought was possible. Over a 20-year period with my good friend, we started recording what could only be released now. Not a second sooner. What came of this musical *conglomeration* was either lightyears ahead of its time or an ancient art left to be dug up somewhere in the distant future. So here it is, me Jeff

Worley, my brother Chris Worley, and our good friend James "Virgil" Hamilton in a trio that came to be called Super V. Why Super V? Over the years people thought that 'Super V' meant super Virgil. On stage Virgil would correct them and say, "I'm the V, and they make it super!" and point to me and my brother. The songs are self-explanatory but expect to use your entire brain to decode them! With this book we grace the audience with a starter explanation to this in-depth material. You are welcome! And if any of you out there find this material to be offensive, we find your offense offensive! So, we are even.

My brother Chris and I loved Virgil as if he were a third Worley brother. There was a brotherhood that was only seen in a World War II movie, with no brother is left behind. We had always discussed, "What are we going to do with this?" There were always talks of showing it to the world 'tomorrow' but unfortunately tomorrow never came. Because my great friend is no longer on this Earth, I know the time is now. Without any

further ado: Thanks for the memories,
thanks for the music, thanks for the laughs,
and thanks for the inspiration. This is for
you Brother. Love you and may you rest
(dance) in heaven.

All Hail Super V! -

Psychobabble

Psycho Babble is a duality straight from Virgil. One thing you need to know, Virgil was an Army Ranger Captain, college graduate, and the kind of person that was so smart in a weird way it was scary. One part of this song describes a weekend tragedy witnessing the death of a fellow soldier, the other part of this song is taken from various scenarios in Virgil's head when his co-worker continued to give him crap!

Hockey mask and bush axe danglin' in my hand

There's trained black widows crawlin' in the sand

I drank my scotch-whiskey and kill 'em with my hand

I'll twist off your head and stretch it like a long rubber band

Evil eye, sinister grin

You don't wanna be in some psycho skin

(Chorus)

Psycho babblin', Psycho babble

He's a Psycho babblin' fool

Psycho babblin', Psycho babble

He's a Psycho babblin' fool

You ain't there, it's in your eyes

I can see you're not ready to die

Just one look is all it takes

To see if you're there for heaven's sakes!

I hear voices just like you

But mine don't tell me what to do!

Ghost and goblins roam your land
But I ain't afraid of the boogey man!

I got a theory that can't be beat
It's call packin' plenty of heat!

(Chorus)

What do you think is wrong with me?
What do I know what is wrong with you.

You got problems, I do too!
I'm just a psycho babblin' fool!

I ain't makin' fun cuz I'm crazy too!

I'll crazy your ass till you're black and blue!

Crazy as hell, just like you!

Do you wanna go we'll act like fools!

Lose them marbles then you'll pay

Electric shock therapy is here to stay!

He's too stupid to breathe through his nose

Caught him wearin' a pair of panty hose

Found poor Leonard out in the yard

Ain't got a full deck, he's missing a card!

(Chorus)

(Autobiography)

They say I'm crazy in a pretty world

I say I'm ugly 'cause I don't get a girl

I'm unusual can't you see?

That's why they call me Super V

Yeah!

We got to groove, and we got to get down!

We shake this place till it hits the ground!

I'm an artist but I ain't no Prince!

I've got two dollars, but I've got no sense!

Come take my picture, come look at me!

The craziest thing you've ever seen!

(chorus)

I'm Super V... *Yeah!*

There ain't none like me!

I'm Super V... *Yeah!*

A one man catastrophe!

I'm Super V... *Yeah!*

You can't keep up with me!

I'm Super V... *Yeah!*

A car wreck, come look and see!

I'm Captain Virgil, call me Super V!

It doesn't matter what you think of me!

You say you're worried about my mind

One thing's for certain, you're wasting your time!

You're wasting your time!

Pardon me for what I might say

I'm going to rock it each and every way!

You come and see me for what I might wear

It doesn't matter 'cause I don't care!

(Repeat chorus)

*Look at me, I don't care, I don't care about
the clothes I wear!*

*The clothes I wear don't make me! *

*The clothes I wear ain't Super V! *

*I was down but I shot up! *

*I'll run you over like a god damn truck!

Some say I don't mind!

Some say I'm super fine!

I'm Super V... Yeah!

El Dorado

El Dorado comes from a poem written by Virgil called "The Fountain of Youth". He showed it to me and my brother. We had no idea what the hell he was talking about, but we immediately started throwing out ideas. The music came immediately! Sometimes that's just how it was!

Ridin' along with my three amigos

There's a mirage dancing on my mind

Carrying on like there's no tomorrow

Who knows what's out there that I will find

Stay on my side even in the curve

Slippery when wet tryin' not to swerve

Stay on the gas pedal don't let up

Take a drink of coffee and fill my cup

Gonna sleep all day
Gonna drive all night

(Chorus)
Goin' down the road to El Dorado
Gonna take a trip way back in time

Gotta give her something that she can
swallow
This much fun it must be a crime

I found that fountain and took a drink
I thought there was nothing that I couldn't
think
I felt myself younger than before

My back was straight, and I wasn't sore

The moral of the story is sad but true
There's a fountain out there for you

It might be right up a road
If you don't look then you'll never know

Gonna sleep all day!*
Gonna drive all night

(Chorus)

Seal Pup

After watching a National Geographic special, Virgil handed me a small essay of his thoughts on the killing of seal pups in the Arctic. He wanted us to write a song about it. On one side were the poachers that would strip them of their fur just for the money it brought while wastefully discarding the carcass. On the other side were the Eskimos who still savagely beat the seal pup's brains out but used all parts of the animal for their survival. Either way the seal pup got its brains beat out. What are your thoughts on this controversial subject? Here's Super V's!

Way up North, where it gets real cold

The men up there ain't got no souls

They kill baby seals

They do it for kicks

They poke 'em in the eye

With their eye pokin' sticks!

Wife wants to leave me

Children hate my guts

Sherriff got red, gonna lock me up

'cuz I killed that hod damn mother sucking
seal pup!

Go ahead and waste a meal

Just to hear it squeal!

How does that dick glove feel?!

(Chorus)

TO KILL!

SEAL PUP!

Strip 'em, rip 'em down to their feet!

When you poke 'em make it neat!

Reach down and grab that fur

Hear that thud, make you wallet purr!

Kick 'em, beat 'em till they're all dead

Poke the eyes out of their head!

Bash in the side of their head!

Squeal no more, now they're dead!

Bludgeon in his head

Beat him till he's dead

Do it 'cause you want to hear

(Chorus)

I rip as many as I can

While they lay asleep on the sand

Make a toast as I spill their guts

Most people see that I'm nuts!

Split them open where they lay

Do it now and earn your pay!

Do it first the old fashion way

Do it now, do it today!

Go ahead and waste a meal!

How does that dick glove feel?

Bludgeon him in his head

Kill him until he's dead

TO KILL!

SEAL PUP!

TO KILL!

SEAL PUP!

WHACK 'EM, BEAT 'EM, WHACK 'EM
ALL!

WHACK 'EM, BEAT 'EM, CAUSE
THEIR SMALL!

WHACK 'EM, BEAT 'EM, WHACK 'EM
ALL!

WHACK 'EM, BEAT 'EM, CAUSE
THEIR SMAAAAAAAAAAAAAALL!

SEAL PUP!

Cannibal Chicken

*After searching for almost 10 years to find
the fitting music that would go with these
lyrics, a cheap keyboard with a simple
prerecorded track of "The Wedding March"
written by Felix Mendelssohn in 1842,
hatched this glorious egg.*

(Chorus)

Everything he sees is finger lickin'

Eats everything including other chickens

My little rooster he's a red and kickin'

He's one damn mean cannibal chicken!

He killed my dog, ate my cat

Mauled and raped my rabbit fur hat

Caught in the closet with my wife's dress

Got caught floggin', what an awful mess

Peckers big and hard just for stickin'
Sharp little beak is just for pickin'!

He's one of a kind, a little DOMINICKER
One legged rooster, he's a real ass kicker!

(Chorus)

Ain't got a bone, he'll eat a can
Eat little children, he'll eat a man

Omnivorous bird, he's a real worm eater
He's got a pecker and a peter!

Robbed 10 chickens with a gun

Ate 10 more, just for fun!

He's a time-bomb, and it's a tickin'

He's my little bitty cannibal chicken

(Chorus)

I Should Have Never Left the House

This song should relate to every person on earth no matter where you're from. At least once in your life you have muttered these fateful words... "I should have never left the house!"

Found myself in a bad situation

You know it ain't the very first time

I thought I picked a safe location

Somewhere they could never find

All my life I've been walking a straight line

Been a good boy most of the time!

Sing in church, knocked me off my feet now

I help old ladies across the street

How nice can I be?

T.R.O.U.B.L... V!

(Chorus)

I should have never ever left the house!

I should have never ever left the house!

Slap me down and shut my mouth!

I should have never ever left the house!

WOOOOOOOO!!

One time he had a girlfriend

And knew just what he would do

Blue lights they came a flashin'

She's fifteen and he's twenty-two!

That spells:

T.R.O.U., T.R.O.U.B.L....V!

(Chorus)

(Gage Worley age 5)

"Where do you think you're goin'?!" Hey,
Virgil, where you think you goin'?!! Hey!
Where you think you goin'?

(Chorus)

UGLY

Depending on how old you are this is a very old chant that was traded back and forth from one side to the other at sporting events, but no doubt ending in many fights. It was one of those things that was hiding in plain sight. We had the chorus down, but we still needed the rest of the lyrics. I jokingly told Virgil to go stand in the mirror and write the rest! He looked at me and said, "Good idea!"

You're so ugly, you could stop a clock

Hands so big they could bust cinderblocks

Your hair weave is like fiberglass

10 acres wouldn't cover your fat ass

Double bags if you please

Ugly to the bone is your disease

Stop a rhino at 20 feet
Welding goggles, they can't be beat!

My retinas burned when I looked your way
Had to wear patches for 14 days

(Chorus)
U. G. L. Y.
You ain't got no alibi
You ugly, yeah you ugly
(repeat)

Your skin feels like alligator hide
Everything you eat, it must be fried!

Hair so oily, what a shine!

Owning mirrors is your big crime!

Thirty weight hairdo, a wide-ass load

Kissing them lips like kissing a toad!

Paper bag wouldn't help your looks

I can judge the cover of your book

Ugly stick won't set you free

You got beat with the whole damn tree!

(Chorus)

You're so ugly you can stop the sun

Looking at you it makes me run!

(Chorus)

*Baby I love you and there is nothing I wouldn't do. **

*But baby, you've got ugly written all over you**

But even uglies give up good lovin' too!

*That's why I'm singin this little song about me and you too! **

Baby I Love You

*Instead of starting with lyrics and creating
music around them, this song started with a
little guitar riff played by Virgil. The V loved
to play guitar, but was not very good at it,
God bless his soul. But that didn't stop him!
He would play an A note all night long! For
about 10 years he would play this riff
continuously, but that was all there was to it.
One fateful night he sang on top of the lick
"Baby I Love You!" If a Neanderthal were
to write a love song this would be it!*

We just met two hours ago

Saw King Kong down at the picture show

She was my queen

I hope she was clean

The damn'dest woman that I have ever seen!

She didn't care

If people would stare

Stare at her purple… at her purple hair

She was mean

She was obscene

She was a ruler, she was a rulin' machine

(Chorus)

Baby I love you, I hope that you love me
too!

So why don't we screw!

Cuz I love you!

She said yes

But I said no

She wanted to do it down at the picture
show

It was so dark down in my seat

Her tattoo's, they were really neat

My hands were wet

I started to sweat

I told her baby you've seen nothin' yet

She was rude

But I was crude

She said yeah babe I'm a freaky dude

(Chorus)

Come on baby, baby, yeah!

(Chorus)

Crack-Cocaine

A simple common-sense observance retold by Super V on the pitfalls of drug use.

Loss my teeth, sold my leg

Got no money, gonna make me beg

Sold my car, lost my shirt

Smoke a little crack just like a jerk

Burnt my tongue and it turned red

My teeth fell out of my head

(Chorus)

Fire it up, feel no pain

Smoke a little crack-cocaine

Funny thing is it make you feel fine

While that shit fucks up your mind!

My nose is glowing, burnin red

My teeth fell out of my head!

I need to go out and buy some more

Even if I have to be a whore!

I smoked it up as fast as I could

I thought I shouldn't, but I knew I would!

(Chorus)

When it's gone I lose my mind

Ain't no egg in the world to find

My nose is stopped up, my pipes in hand

I'm in search of the Easter egg man

Fire it up at light speed

A big ol' egg is all you need!

(Chorus)

Smoke that shit and you'll turn blind!

Lose your teeth and your behind!

Eat your mind right out of your head!

Make your heart stop, you'll end up dead!

Crack-Cocaine!

Hey Big!

This song is slightly unique in the sense that it came from a distant memory and has a dual meaning. Virgil one night witnessed a fatal car accident involving a Cadillac full of intoxicated Mexicans. My brother and I were so taken by the story and subject matter that 20 minutes later we had a song! The moral of this story is that no matter how big you think you are, there's always someone or something bigger. So basically, this song is about the "Grim Reaper" coming to get all of us.

Juan and Julio, cousins in back

Packed like sardines in a black Cadillac

Through the crossroads, stop ahead!

Flipped ten times, they wound up dead!

Billy badass, his chip turned red

Little miss thang and my best friend in bed

Sent her packing, her ass in her hands

Hey Big! I'm your man! Yeah, I'm your man!

(Chorus)

Hey Big! I'm your man!

What's up Big? I eat from a trash can!

Hey Big! I'm your man!

What's up Big? I eat from a trash can!

Let me tell you man, I'm so big!

I'm bigger than a tractor trailer rig!

I'm bigger than a locomotive diesel train

I'm bigger than a 747 plane!

Am I insane?!

(Chorus)

I've got a shadow that's hard to fill

Hey Big! I'm king of this damn hill!

I'm 6 foot 6 and tree top tall!

I knock em dead and watch em fall!

(Chorus)

F.U.K.P.O.D

F.U.K.P.O.D was condensed from 4 pages of what Virgil called "spiritual venting". Come to find out it came from a post gig experience that we're gonna let the song explain.

Coming down the road with a drink in my hand

Jacked sky high, done spent a grand

Coming down the road with a drink in my hand

Busted flat broke, one hell of a man

(chorus)

'Cause I'm fucked up, pissed off, and drunk!

My breath, the bitch said it stunk!

'Cause I'm fucked up, pissed off, and drunk!

Well that ain't the only that stunk!

Coming down the road with a joint in my
hand

Got no direction to the promise land

Got no money for no gasoline

Put it all in the poker machine!

Hope by God that I'm stoned!

'Cause baby I'll find my own way home

(Chorus)

break it down one more time…!

SHOOOOOWEEEYOOOWEEEEOOOOWEEE
OOOOWWWEEEOOOO X8

"PICK YOUR FEET UP!

WHAT'S WRONG WITH YOU?

ARE YOOOOU CRAZYYY?!!

YAK, YAK, YAK, COW!!!"

Smoke Dope

Super V says:

"Please legalize God's greatest gift to Mankind!"

It starts out a helpless seed

Burn up some of that evil weed

Gets some newspaper and some glue

Roll up a fat doob for me and you!

Burn that sucker, let it set you free!

Sweet leaf is grown here for you and me!

Eat it in some brownies or homebrewed tea!

Fire that sucker till it make you scream!

(Chorus)

Marijuana! (x4)

Smoke dope! (x4)

Smoke that dope!

Smoke dope! (x4)

Don't you worry your head a bit

This dope is some far out shit!

Fucks you up, really good

Take your clothes off, make you run through the woods!

Bust yo ass, then you'll see

This skunk bud will put you on your knees

Hurt you, knock your ass to the ground

This shit grows 6 feet out of the ground!

(Chorus)

Ohhh yeah! Smoke-o El Loco!

It's a conspiracy against Mother Nature is what it is!

A little harmless innocent little weed, ain't nothing to smoking a joint by yourself!

Ain't hurtin' nobody! It ain't no harm, but it is in the eyes of the law.

Hell, I'll I want to do is smoke me a joint ever now and then.

All I want to do is fire it up!

Go ahead!

Fire it up!!!

Maybe mother's milk, or daddy's cream

Some say its evil, in your dreams!

Smoke it till you split, at the seams

Fire that sucker till it makes you scream!

(repeat chorus until you pass out)

V.D.

Virgil Dammit?

Totin' guns, carrying knives

I'm the deadliest man alive

Run and hide, do or die, I've got the devil
right by my side

Call me pissed, call me mean

I'm the damn'dest thing you've ever seen

Come and see

Watch me go

I'll tell you things you've never did known!

I was raised up in the south

I am the bad taste in your mouth!

I said yeah! Yeah! Yeah! Yeah!
Yeahhaayahhh

(Chorus)
I am the V. D.!
I am the V. D.!
I am the V. D.
And I am very, very dangerous! Yeah!

All the women's grin when I walk by
Some of them break down and cry
Looks so good
Smells so sweet
Ain't nothin' much I won't eat!

I've been around for heaven's sakes
Tijuana Mexico takes the cake!
On vacation I blew a tire

And I fell into a ring of fire!

I was raised up in the south

I am the bad taste in your mouth!

I said yeah!, Yeah! Yeah!

(Chorus)

You know what I'm saying?

You know what I'm talking about?

Don't call me no vulgar display,

What do you mean calling me a vulgar display?!

I file a discharge on your ass bitch! You know why?

Well I'll tell you why!

Cuz my name is VIRGIL DAMMIT!

(Chorus)

21st Century Redneck

*Virgil, Chris, and I contrived this
masterpiece one night after pondering this
one specific subject. The one thing we all
had in common, you see, is that we come
from a small rural town where the further
you went out in the country, the more things
started to go awry. The souls out there were
generous and loving but these people
decided to live on their own terms. Let the
song explain for you.*

Painted my car with a paint brush

Toilet's backed up, granny can't flush!

Thangs is tough, thangs is hard!

Chickens is roosting in my back yard!

Blue jeans hanging down to my crack

Come payday I'll buy a six pack!

I might be white but I ain't trash!

I like fried tatters and corn beef hash!

I've got a truck, I've got a gun

Gonna go out and have some fun!

Attitude, feelin' rude

That's why they call me…

That's why they call me…

(Chorus)

21st Century, 21st , Century, 21st , Century
redneck lives!

21st Century, 21st , Century, 21st , Century
redneck lives!

I'm so red I almost glow
You can smell the red with your nose!

I can play a beer can like a Jew's harp
Country fired caviar, we call it carp!

Think of the world if it was red
A lot more licks upside the head!

Orange hair on a G.I. Joe
You wanna fight? Come on baby let's go!

Suicide, Astroglide,
My car seats are Naugahyde!

Dad's in jail, for raising hell!
My sister's on the corner, her booty's for
sale!

(Chorus)

I want to tell you about a redneck.

Anybody can be a redneck, anyone can jump red.

All it takes is a pair of jumper cables to jump red!

WOOOOOOOOOOOOOOOOO!

Jimmy Swagger, he's my man!

I watch him every chance, that I can!

If he can't do it, nobody can!

He's a 21st century preacher man!

I read about him in the STAR!

I think Jimmy took her just a little too far!

(Chorus)

Burnt-Monkey"s?

Dedicated to

Lt. John (Jack) Trowbridge, U.S.A.F

(YouTube him)

You must have been living under a freaking rock if you have not heard about the 1949 Roswell, New Mexico UFO crash. This is Super V's take on the situation: No aliens crashed in the desert, they were monkeys! Let me explain. Virgil conjectured that a Japanese Fugo bomb was the answer. That was a single nuclear bomb placed it in a sort of weather balloon manned by monkeys destined for the United States. But the balloon had gotten trapped in the high atmospheric winds for 4 years and eventually crashing in the New Mexican desert. The UFO and alien conspiracy were just cover for the fact of how close we were to being irradiated.

*Damn! Did you see that! That's a UFO! Bet
there's aliens on board!*

Monkey strapped to a Saturn V

Ass drawed tight, gonna take a ride

He's in orbit on a one-way flight

Mission control is in command tonight

UFO crash, they said so

UFO crash, no hell no!

No hell no!

Standing out in broad daylight

Did you see that terrible sight?

(Chorus)

Burnt burnt, burnt monkey's

Burnt burnt, burnt monkey's

Burnt burnt, burnt monkey's

Burnt burnt, burnt monkey's

Hit the ground with a splat

Doin' it all for Mr. Green Hat

Little bitty alien's lyin' on the ground

Said it were monkeys that were found

Uncle Sam said this case closed!

What really happened no one knows!

No one knows!

Wrap them up in clean rags

Zip them up in body bags!

(Chorus)

*"Hello? Is this the Roswell police
department? There's something crashed out
in my pasture! It's scaring my cows!"*

George saved Roswell and the nation today

Truman told the Generals just what to say

Keep them quiet, silence them all

UFO crash is what we saw!

Pile that shit in Hangar 18

Never again will it be seen!

Alien flight school flip flop flunky

That's who was the real burnt monkey's!

(Chorus)

If you say a word about it,

you will end up in deep shit!

<u>COWORKER!!!</u>

*In a state of fury one evening, Virgil
grabbed the microphone and started
screaming this out. My brother and I wrote
the music with much haste!*

(Chorus)

COWORKER!

COWORKER!

COWORKER!

COWORKER!

Co-Worker, co-worker, help me please

I'm throwing up on my knees

Pull me up by my bootstraps

Trim my sails, pull back my boot flaps!

OOOOOOHHH   YEEAAHHHH!

Co-worker, co-worker, where you've been?!

Been down town to do it again?!

Doin' it, doin' it, it ain't no sin!

If you still got the box that it came in!

(Chorus)

Co-worker! Co-worker! Kiss my ass and lick
it clean! You bubblegum chewing dizzy
bitch, you're so damn mean!

You plaid coat wearing line-dancing fool!
You're sick and mean, you are so damn
cruel!

Co-Worker! Co-Worker! Help me in here!

Are you happy or are you queer?!

Plaster my ass all over the wall

Nail my nut-sack to the floor!

And give me … some more!

(Repeat chorus 17 times or until sick or in fit
of rage)

Party! Party! Party!

One night Virgil was unknowingly taken into a gay club by two girls. What transpired is described below by Super V's extremely unique perspective.

Swing your partner dosey doe

Swing her around and don't let her go

Texas star to the right

Swing her all day and party all night!

(Chorus)

If you wanna cum and party, gonna shut you down

If you cum into my party, burn it to the ground!

Party! Party! Party!

Just… because we can!

Party! Party! Party!

I'm the party man!

Jump, scream, and shout come on give me a
hand

Party! Party! Party! I'm the party man

Party all day and party all night!

Let's spin some jams, spin it out of sight!

Feel, the grove, yeah! You got it, you got it
so tight!

Party on down, yeah, party until you get in a
fight!

(Chorus)

Blue lights flashing music it comes alive!

Feel the music groovin', feel it movin' down
your thighs!

The room is flashing and a bashin', yeah it's
in a rave!

If you come to my party don't act your age!

(Chorus)

Photo by Meg Wallace

Thank you to all of our fans and friends for all of your love and support. Thanks for the laughs, pointing and gasping.

Book cover design: Jeff & Lisa Worley

For more information visit:

www.worleythepirate.com

Like us @ facebook.com/WorleythePirate

Follow us on IG @ Worley_the_pirate_productions

& worleythepirateart

Kuckaburro

[kuck-ah-bur-oh] *noun*

1. A misspelled word for an Australian kingfisher, *Dacelo gigas*, having a loud, harsh cry that resembles laughter.
2. A word that Super V uses in reference to a dingleberry.

Made in the USA
Columbia, SC
17 March 2019